LIFE AFTER YOUR LOVER WALKS OUT:

A PRACTICAL GUIDE

By LYNDA BEVAN

THE 10-STEP EMPOWERMENT SERIES

Life After Your Lover Walks Out: A Practical Guide

Book #1 in the 10-Step Empowerment Series

Copyright © 2007 Lynda Bevan. All Rights Reserved.

No part of this publication reproduced, transmitted in any form or by any means, electronic, mechanical, photocopying, recording, or other otherwise, or stored in a retrieval system, without the prior written consent of the publisher.

First Edition: January 2007

Library of Congress Cataloging-in-Publication Data

```
Bevan, Lynda.
   Life after your lover walks out : a practical guide /
by Lynda Bevan.
         p. cm. --  (10-step empowerment series)
   Includes bibliographical references and index.
   ISBN-13: 978-1-932690-26-2 (pbk. : alk. paper)
   ISBN-10: 1-932690-26-3 (pbk.)
  1.  Man-woman relationships. 2.  Separation (Psychol-
ogy) 3.  Adjustment (Psychology)  I. Title. II. Series:
Bevan, Lynda. 10-step empowerment series.

   HQ801.B496 2007
   155.9'3--dc22
                                     2006017301
```

Published by:
Loving Healing Press
5145 Pontiac Trail
Ann Arbor, MI 48105
USA

http://www.LovingHealing.com or
info@LovingHealing.com
Fax +1 734 663 6861

Loving Healing Press

What People Are Saying About: *Life After Your Lover Walks Out*

"The dissolution of relationships, especially of the romantic variety, leaves the abandoned partner dazzled, depleted, and traumatized. In such a state of mind, one gropes for concise, hands-on no-nonsense guidance. Regrettably, most self-help literature is bloated, narcissistic, and off-topic. If you know someone who has just been painfully dumped by their significant other—buy them this booklet."

—Sam Vaknin, *Malignant Self Love: Narcissism Revisited*.

"Lynda Bevan delivers what she promises in the title of the book: it is a practical guide and a no-nonsense approach. Her descriptions of the experiences are palpable."

—Chin Tao, LMFT

"This is a well thought out, useful little book that is an excellent guide for those recovering from a broken long-term relationship."

—Robert Rich, MSc, PhD, M.A.P.S.,

"Nowadays there are too many books about adult loving relationships, but they usually are generic and abstract descriptions. This book is different because it moves to specificity and provides concrete steps to overcome a disrupting episode in our lives."

—Carlos J. Sanchez, MA, Family Therapist

"A hands-on guide, Bevan leads us through the stages of loss and mourning, then foster movement towards integration and the creation of healthy new relationships."

—Carolyn Crimmins, Psy.D

"This book is succinct and in clear language for the lay (non-mental health professional) reader to understand. Bevan has real-life experience in the area of loss and 'rebuilding' her life and self-esteem in the face of traumatic experiences such as being abandoned by a partner."

—Margaret M. Mustelier, Psy.D.

"An excellent tool to help persons move on after the end of a relationship. *Life After Your Lover Walks Out* highlights the common cognitive distortions and exaggerated emotions and urges the reader to examine their actions and how they perpetuate their feeling of loss. Through the use of introspective questions the book invites the reader to take a journey of self examination in order to accept the loss and to reengage in life."

—Ian Landry, MA, MSW, Case Manager

Table of Contents

Introduction v

Step 1: Falling apart / shock 1
"What can I do to get him/her back?" 1
The Second Day 6
Emotions 7
Left You For Someone Else 8
Outgrowing The Other Person 10
Children of the Partnership 12

Step 2: Why Is This Happening To Me? 17
"I am unlovable" 17
"I deserve to be unhappy" 19
"No one can love me?" 19
"God is paying me back" 20
"I can't keep a relationship" 20

Step 3: Fear of the Future 23
Being alone 23
Surviving on Less Money 24
Being on the rebound: Lack of trust for any future relationships 28

Step 4: The Grieving Process 37
Guilt 38
Anger 39
Giving in and giving up 41
Fear 42
Seeing someone through rose-tinted glasses 46
Loneliness 47
Things not to do: 50

Step 5: Acceptance and Realisation 53
Take a risk 53

    Acceptance 54

Step 6: Family and Friends 57
    Your Support System 57
    The Ladder of Recovery 59

Step 7: Moving On 59
    Finding New Goals 63

Step 8: Reinvestment / Restructure 63
    Dependent vs. Healthy Relationships 67
    Priorities 69

Step 9: Look to the Future 71
    How do you plan a future? 71
    Deciding what you want: 71

Step 10: A New You 73
    New relationships 75
    Letting go of the past 77

About the Author 78

Bibliography 81

Index 83

About our Series Editor, Robert Rich, Ph.D.

Loving Healing Press is pleased to announce Robert Rich, Ph.D. as Series Editor for the *10-Step Empowerment Series*. This exciting new series conveys practical guides written by seasoned therapists for solving real-life problems.

Robert Rich, M.Sc., Ph.D., M.A.P.S., A.A.S.H. is a highly experienced counseling psychologist. His web site www.anxietyanddepression-help.com is a storehouse of helpful information for people suffering from anxiety and depression.

Bob is also a multiple award-winning writer of both fiction and non-fiction, and a professional editor. His writing is displayed at www.bobswriting.com. You are advised not to visit him there unless you have the time to get lost for a while.

Three of his books are tools for psychological self-help: *Anger and Anxiety: Be in charge of your emotions and control phobias*, *Personally Speaking: Single session email therapy*, and *Cancer: A personal challenge*. However, his philosophy and psychological knowledge come through in all his writing, which is perhaps why three of his books have won international awards, and he has won many minor prizes. Dr. Rich currently resides at Wombat Hollow in Australia.

The New Horizons in Therapy Series

- Got parts? An Insider's Guide to Managing Life Successfully with Dissociative Identity Disorder, by ATW
- Got parts? Companion: A Workbook of Understanding and Hope
- Coping with Physical Loss and Disability: A Workbook, by Rick Ritter, MSW
- Enfrentando la Discapacidad y el Deterioro Físico: Un Manual, by Rick Ritter, MSW
- Why Good People Make Bad Choices: How You Can Develop Peace Of Mind Through Integrity, by Charles Allen

Loving Healing Press is dedicated to producing books about innovative and rapid therapies which redefine what is possible for healing the mind and spirit.

Introduction

The experience of your lover walking out is devastating. It creates a situation where the abandoned partner is left to their own devices, in order to find out:

- Why this has occurred
- What they could have done to prevent it
- How to retrieve it
- How to 'move on'

This book clearly identifies the thoughts and feelings that emerge during this difficult time, and offers immediate options, suggestions and ideas on how to cope with these destructive emotions. The chapters are called 'Steps' and begin 'when your lover walks' out to the final 'Step,' becoming a new you.

The emptiness, despair and fears experienced during this time are openly discussed. No stone is left unturned. This process is an essential element in moving on from a **negative emotional experience** to a **positive emotional outcome**. Any person, from whatever background, age or culture, who has been 'unceremoniously' dumped, will experience certain negative thought processes. As this book reveals, these are not unique to you but are universal activities. It provides the reader with realistic options on how to handle each Step on the way to emotional recovery.

The book can be read in less than two hours. It is deliberately written in a short, condensed style. This is in order to avoid wading through copious amounts of case studies that, in my opinion, are inconsequential to the abandoned partner during this difficult period. People in this situation are only interested in learning how to live through the emotional and practical issues that arise. This book searches the core of the problem and supports and directs the abandoned partner to a satisfactory, practical and emotional conclusion.

Life After Your Lover Walks Out: A Practical Guide, is a down to earth, no nonsense approach to the emotional turmoil when this happens.

It encourages the reader to open their eyes, accept what has happened and to view themselves, their life, and their future in a positive way.

Step 1 Falling Apart / Shock

Your lover has walked out. What you have feared for yourself has come to pass. You are left alone. Your friend, your lover, your companion for many years has just walked out of your home and out of your life.

- You feel numb
- Your feel helpless
- You feel alone

Unanswerable questions fly around in your head:

- How has this happened?
- Why have you come to this?
- Could you have prevented it?
- What can you do to get him/her back

"What can I do to get him/her back?"

This is the first thought most of us have when someone we still love and want walks out:

- You can't bear the loss of your loved one
- You can't see a future without this person
- You are desperate and will do anything to mend the relationship
- You frantically try to contact your now-ex, phoning, writing, asking mutual friends to intervene on your behalf so you can talk with each other, to 'make your beloved see sense'
- You feel you cannot function without your partner

This list is typical for people who still want to hang on to their relationship and their partner.

Other people, however, might give a huge sigh of relief when their partner walks out. The tension and dissatisfaction experienced by the couple in the relationship has finally reached a conclusion. The decision to separate might be the result of a well thought out process with both partners satisfied that the relationship should end.

If the separation is because one of the partners cannot continue in the relationship for whatever reason then the partner who leaves might feel:

- All the blame is on their shoulders
- Guilty that they caused the relationship to end
- Angry at being 'pushed out'
- Want revenge on their partner because they feel they have been treated unfairly

Whatever the reason for the separation, when it comes you are astounded when it actually happens. You might have known for some time that it was going to happen but when the time comes you are shocked, dazed, and disoriented. It's difficult to take in what's happening to you.

When a partner leaves initially you might heave a sigh of relief, but if you believe you are still in love with that person then you are shattered, emotionally drained, stuck on the path of your life, and empty inside. The life you spent with your partner swims before your eyes and fills your mind remembering only the good times. You search frantically in your mind to remember bad things, but search as you will it is difficult to remember anything that couldn't have been dealt with successfully—now

Step 1 – Falling Apart/Shock

that you look back. So, why didn't you handle things differently?

Family and friends try to help—to no avail. It seems that you are locked inside your head and No one can enter your mind to unshackle the thoughts that are drowning you. Everything you see, touch, and feel is second rate to your yearning for the past. You are alone. You may be surrounded by well meaning family and friends, but nothing stops the ache and emptiness. You believe you are doomed to be unhappy forever.

This is the worst stage in the process of grieving for your partner, in my opinion. You cease to function on a 'normal' level. You hear people around you saying that 'you will get over it' or 'there are plenty more fish in the sea.' But to you there is only one 'fish' and s/he just left you.

You find it difficult to concentrate and take in information. You look to the people who are close to you to provide you with the answers that you need to survive, e.g. "S/he'll be back!' or, alternatively, "It's all for the best," but you don't want to and simply can't think that way.

You somehow get through the first day after s/he has left. Family and friends gather around you and you systematically repeat to them the story of how this has happened and relive the final hours prior to the walkout. You shed endless tears of remorse at your part in the split-up. People come and go to your home offering you comforting words and support.

Some people who have been deserted by their partner have no family or friends that they can turn to at this difficult time. They have no supportive safety net to help them through this process of change. We all react in different ways:

- Withdrawing into yourself (can't talk to anyone)
- Depression (feeling helpless and unwanted)
- Isolation (want to be left alone)
- Loneliness (can't share their problem with others)
- Remorse (regret that the relationship has broken down, particularly if you are the cause)
- Anxiety (feeling panicky with No one to turn to)
- Fear (scared of the future)
- Unworthy (always believed the relationship would end)
- No self-confidence (would rather hide away than face people)
- Secretive (hide it as long as possible. Cannot confront the issue)
- Ashamed (what will people think of me?)
- Failed (my partner is with someone else. I have, therefore, failed in my relationship)

These are just some of the possible emotions that are felt by the partner who does not want to end the relationship.

The partner who is left behind feels alone. If you have children, the house is quiet after they have gone to bed. All your supportive friends have vanished to their own homes and lives; to their own partners. You are left alone with your thoughts. Day becomes night and you experience the loss more keenly. It is like a hole in the pit of your stomach that nothing will fill. There is a hole in your heart left in your partner's shape that No one will ever be able to fit into. It is a void. A vacuum.

Step 1 – Falling Apart/Shock

You try and watch the television; there are endless chores to be done but you can't face doing anything that might temporarily distract you from thinking about your loss.

You are your own torturer: regurgitating situations and events that prodded the break-up. You chastise both yourself and your partner for leaving you. You are locked in this state of having to keep your loss in your mind, despite the pain it causes you. You become illogical believing that if you keep your partner in your mind you will somehow send a message of your deep regret bringing your love back to you. You walk around the house and everything that you look at reminds you of him/her.

- The color scheme of your home
- The furniture your partner brought or decorating that s/he did
- The food in the cupboards and fridge that s/he liked

Wherever you turn you are reminded that s/he doesn't love you anymore and has gone.

Finally you climb the stairs to go to bed. You trundle along to the bathroom to clean your teeth and there is his/her toothbrush standing up straight and looking at you as if nothing has happened.

The knot of fear and hurt twists in your stomach. The pain is excruciating.

You undress and hang up your clothes. Staring at you from inside the closet or wardrobe are most of the clothes your partner has left behind, perhaps to collect at some future time. You touch them lovingly with tears running down your cheeks.

This is like a bad dream—please let me wake up and have everything be all-right again. If only you had paid attention to the rising tensions, valued your partner, or talked to them more often. You feel it is all your fault and you cannot forgive yourself. You get into the big double bed and are immediately aware of the empty space beside you. His/her pillows are still there—you cannot bear to take them off the bed as it would be too final. You can smell your ex-partner in the bed and on the sheets. It is a distinctive smell and, once again you are in floods of tears hugging the pillows and praying to God, "please let my lover return."

You eventually drop off to sleep exhausted.

The Second Day

If you are the partner who has left or been kicked out, then you may have no alternative but to move in with a parent or even take up temporary residence at a motel room.

Then morning comes, and the minute you open your eyes you realize that the previous day was not a bad dream but in fact all too real. You are alone. This is the second day of your new life and you hate it. You have nothing to look forward to. You may as well be dead.

Somehow, you accomplish the needs of the children on automatic pilot. They go to school and once again that sharp pain is there locking you into a world of hurt.

You try and do your chores; you try to act normal when friends and neighbors call. You feel you are cocooned in a surreal place of your own making and can barely hear what anyone is saying. You move in slow motion. People are talking to you and you cannot take anything in. If they say that 'you are better off without him/her,' it isn't what you want to hear so you block

Step 1 – Falling Apart/Shock 7

it out. Nothing that is helpful penetrates your mind at this stage. You can only think, 'I want him/her back.'

Alternately, if you have a job, then you will have to go through the routine of a day's work at the office or factory. You will have to concentrate on the daily tasks with a load of emotional issues on your mind that will distract you. Even if you choose to update your manager on what is happening in your personal life and they are sympathetic, the output of work still has to be completed.

Emotions

We go through a myriad of emotions during this time:

- Shock/Numbness
- Anger at the other person and yourself
- Hate
- Guilt – what have I done to deserve this?
- Disorganization, confusion—can't think straight
- Fear—what am you are going to do?
- Poor decision making—afraid of making the wrong choice
- Apathy
- Purposeless—no point in living
- Disinclined to be involved with anyone and anything – other than attempts to get him/her back
- Neglect of your appearance and home (poor self-care)
- Anxiety
- Depression

For some, this stage can last a long time. Most often, it lasts for a few days. You keep looking at the clock and waiting for your partner to return. When the phone rings you jump and reach for the receiver in the futile hope that it is him/her. You inevitably experience disappointment after disappointment. Eventually you will accept that your lover is not returning, but it's too soon for that now. You pray to God that He will intervene and spare you any more of this horrible heartache.

You start thinking of the future without your partner and the very thought of this frightens you. You ask yourself:

- How will you cope alone?
- How will you manage financially?
- Are you destined to be unhappy forever?
- Where do you start?
- Will you trust again?

A man looking at a future without his partner might be faced with practical issues: preparing meals, getting the laundry done, dealing with a myriad of service providers for the home, etc.

You may feel able to confide your fears to family and friends, but nothing they say comforts you. However, many people who have experienced such a loss choose to bottle up their emotions and don't feel able to tell anyone.

Left You For Someone Else

Perhaps your partner has left you for someone else.

If you are a woman, then the hatred and anger you feel toward him and his 'bit on the side,' corrodes your thinking. You have visions of your partner making love to this other person, treating them tenderly, doing the simplest of tasks for them. Holding hands, whispering sweet nothings, sharing cares and worries, planning and excited about their future together. You imagine:

Step 1 – Falling Apart/Shock

- This woman sitting in your seat in the car
- This woman touching the clothes you washed and ironed for your partner
- She is touching your partner intimately

Only you should do those things! After all you earned the right by loving him through thick and thin. You were his partner, cook, cleaner, lover, friend, nurse.

If you are a man and have been replaced by another person in your relationship you may have different thoughts whirling around in your mind:

- You will feel affronted because you provided practical and emotional support to your partner during the birth and raising of your children
- You have the image of your partner making love with another man
- Another man may be occupying your place in the home
- You have the image of another man talking with and taking some responsibility for your children
- You will resent another man enjoying your family

Whether male or female, you may feel that whatever it is — you did it. You may ask yourself, *where did I go wrong?* Perhaps you haven't done anything wrong. Maybe you both had outlived your relationship, and the time had come when there was nothing left between you to salvage. It might have been wonderful for most of the years you were together but it has come to a natural conclusion. You ask yourself the question, "Are people really meant to be together forever, 'till death do us part?"

Perhaps you met your partner when you were young. You didn't know much about life and relationships when you first started your life together. You thought you knew everything back then. Later, you realize, you didn't.

Life, marriage, living together and emotional problem solving are not on the school curriculum, so how could you learn it?

Your mind is full of unanswered questions.

- Did you really expect to live your life forever together and, simultaneously, grow emotionally?
- Should you remain with the same person forever?

Outgrowing The Other Person

You might think that no one grows emotionally at the same rate, so what happens if one partner outgrows the other? You ponder and look for alternatives. Maybe it would be more realistic to have a 'marriage contract' that could be renewed every five years! If that were to happen it might make you work harder at your relationship and not take your partner for granted. It might be a good idea to have written in the contract that it should be reviewed annually. You could both draw up an action plan with monthly targets to achieve. Business projects work this way, why not marriage? If these targets are not met then the contract becomes null and void. You search through your mind to find answers to age old problems. Your ideas sound drastic, I know. But hey, anything that will stop this continual hurt is worth thinking about.

These thoughts make you feel worse; you don't want to think that you weren't meant to be together for ever. Nothing you think makes you feel any better.

Step 1 – Falling Apart/Shock

Your confidence has taken a knock.

- You feel ugly
- You feel rejected
- You feel inadequate
- You feel unlovable

You tell yourself *you must be all of these things.*

Your mind is in a whirl you cannot stop thinking and some of the thoughts that fill your mind you don't like and don't want.

Perhaps the reason for the split is that *you* have outgrown *him/her* emotionally and intellectually.

For a woman:

Perhaps he couldn't keep up with you. He might have felt inadequate and unconfident in the relationship. Perhaps you are holding down a full-time responsible job and caring for your family at the same time. What are you—'wonder-woman?'

For a man:

Perhaps you feel held back by your partner? Perhaps you feel your partner has changed and no longer shares your vision of the future? Perhaps your partner resents the fact that you are out at work all day and are always tired in the evenings? Perhaps your partner feels left behind that you put your work before the family?

You are questioning every aspect of yourself and the years you've spent together. Feelings of negativity abound. You cannot smile; you don't act spontaneously; you can feel yourself spiraling down into the abyss. If there are children from this union, you will feel an added responsibility in that you will feel that you must stay strong and in control of the situation in order for them to feel safe.

This state of disbelief is disconcerting but in a strange way somehow safe. You are operating on automatic pilot and getting the necessary tasks done. You are in a daze. You transcend from tears and remorse to becoming numb and stupefied.

You tell yourself that this negative outcome had been inevitable from the start. You have always believed that you aren't worth being loved and cared for — you should have known that the relationship was doomed to failure. After all nothing else has ever worked for you — why should this?

As the days and maybe the weeks pass by, your family and friends begin to worry that you are not coming to terms with the split and may recommend you see your doctor to get help. You don't want medical help; you want your partner back in your arms. Why doesn't anyone understand that simple fact?

Eventually you might be persuaded to see your doctor who will either prescribe anti-depressants or refer you to a Counselor. You might prefer the anti-depressant route and start taking them already convinced they are not going to work — how can they? The tablets won't bring him/her back will they? Alternatively you might welcome the opportunity of sharing your feelings with a Counselor. You may, however, reject both these routes.

Children of the Partnership

During this time, you also have to answer searching questions from the children of the partnership.

Step 1 – Falling Apart/Shock

- Where is daddy/mommy?
- Why isn't s/he here?
- What have you done daddy/mommy to send him/her away?
- What have we done to daddy/mommy to make them leave?

If the kids are lucky and you have the strength, you explain to them that both of you love them dearly but have decided to live in separate houses because, whilst you still like each other, you don't want to live in the same house together anymore and you reassure them that they can see mommy/daddy as often as they want to.

This answer satisfies most children for a little while until they fully realize that the life they once knew is never going to return.

Older children of five years and upwards would probably have a good idea of what is happening in the household and, accepting this fact, should be told the bare bones of the situation. In my experience, older children respond well to the truth and can understand and be supportive during this difficult time.

It is important during a separation or divorce to ensure that the bond between parent and child is not broken. Children need both parents to be involved in their lives so that they can develop physically, mentally and emotionally. The breaking of the bond between parent and child can be traumatic for a child.

The interaction between parents during this difficult time can affect the self-esteem and confidence of their child. Therefore, it is vital to been seen as co-operating with each other, behaving in a civilized manner and respectful of your position as role models for your child.

During this emotional upheaval the dynamics in the household will change dramatically with one parent taking responsibility for the everyday care and nurturing of the child. Seen through the child's eyes, this situation alone can rock their world. The child might feel abandoned by the departed parent. Even though the child is living with only one parent, it is important that the child is able to see and talk with the other parent on a regular basis. Depending on the age of the child and their understanding of the circumstances children can react in the following ways:

- Blaming themselves for the split-up
- Withdrawing into themselves
- Displaying destructive behavior
- Unruly and out of control at school
- Getting poor grades at school
- Tantrums
- Bed-wetting
- Depressive symptoms
- Smoking, drinking and drug
- Leaving school/home when young
- Becoming sexually active or a parent at an early age
- Aggression, delinquency and other anti-social behavior

It is for this, and many other reasons, that parents should keep a close eye on how their child is coping with the current situation. A divorce can have far reaching consequences on a family unit. Trust is an essential element in all relationships and particularly so during a separation or divorce. The decision you both have made to end the marriage should not affect the responsibility you both have toward your child.

Step 1 – Falling Apart/Shock

The bond between parent and child should be a continuing factor throughout their life. I believe it is safe to say that all children of divorced parents will feel some distress at the time of the separation. In most cases, this reaction will fade with the passing of time and with the way both parents handle this situation.

With my own divorce, I decided early on to be as honest as I could with my children. I actively encouraged open communication and trust between us because I believe honesty, trust, and communication are key ingredients for healthy relationships.

Some families might need the assistance of a Counselor trained to identify the stages that a child of separated parents experiences. This service is a valuable asset particularly if the relationship between the parents has irretrievably broken down.

Children and Finances

Needless to say that in the majority of cases, separation or divorce will have a detrimental effect on the finances within the household. This causes problems for the children of the relationship. It limits their options with regard to the following:

- Financial difficulties can limit educational options
- Financial difficulties can limit future health care
- Living on a tighter budget can reduce food luxuries
- Lower socio-economic status (not being able to purchase designer gear, etc., and unable to keep up with the spending trends of friends)
- Fewer opportunities to have outings and holidays

During the process of separation divorce and custody battles, the child's emotional and financial needs must be top priority for both partners.

Good honest, down to earth communication between the child and both parents is especially important in assisting the child to adapt to a new set of circumstances be it financial, physical or emotional.

Quality time spent with your child is the main objective that the departed partner must strive to achieve.

Step 2   Why Is This Happening To Me?

These are just some of the thoughts that may flash through your mind repeatedly when your partner walks out on you:

- I am unlovable
- I deserve to be unhappy
- God is paying me back for all the wrong I have done
- No one can love me
- I can't keep a relationship

"I am unlovable"

Are you? Let's examine the negatives of this belief:

- You can be stubborn or touchy at times
- You can let household chores or the job get the better of you
- You moan, needlessly
- You are too tired, sometimes, to make love
- You spend too much money
- You don't always feel like making an effort with your appearance
- You often don't listen to your partner's viewpoint
- You can't easily 'let go' of a situation
- You blame your partner for problems without just cause

How many of the above can you recognize?

This list is a typical example. However everyone's list will be different and unique to them. You can go on and on with the negatives if you put your mind to it. What is the point of all this chastising? Most 'normal' people are guilty of the negatives you have identified. It's called 'being human.'

Stop looking at all that stuff.

Let's examine the positives:
- You are a decent, all-right, person
- You wouldn't purposefully harm anyone
- You are fair-minded
- You always try to do your best
- You are a good mother/father
- You are a good wife/husband
- You do the household chores as best you can in your circumstances
- You are thoughtful, caring, and understanding
- You try to see the other person's point of view
- You are a good friend
- You are a considerate lover
- You are supportive of your partner's job

This list is a general example and not applicable to everyone. We are all individuals and as such will think and experience different feelings at this time.

How many of the above can you confirm is you?

Concentrate on your good points; realize and accept that your partner has a negative side also. It takes two to argue and two to break-up. Which comes first, 'the chicken or the egg?'

You are in 'the fog of life.' You are depressed and angry and you don't know which emotion is the worse.

Not everyone will agree with these suggested positives. Whatever you feel is accurate is appropriate to you.

"I deserve to be unhappy"

Do you? Let's examine this also. No one deserves to be unhappy. Everyone has the ability to achieve changes that lead to a life of quality.

What have you done that's so bad?

- You may have had several relationships
- Maybe you treated one or two of your relationships badly
- Perhaps you had/have a bad relationship with one or both of your parents
- Maybe you cheated on your partner and they still don't know about it

Unless you are a mass murderer, rapist, or pedophile, you don't deserve to be unhappy. The law takes care of these people — they have their penance to pay society.

"No one can love me?"

Why? Let's examine this universal popular belief:

- If you try to do your best…
- If you are fair to others…
- If you can accept you are not always right…
- If you try to see other people's point of view and allow them their opinion…
- If you know your limitations and bad points and own them…

…Then you are lovable.

Take a look around you at people you know and respect. How are they handling their difficult situations? Do they react badly sometimes? Of course they do, we all do. Forgive yourself and decide to change that aspect of yourself that you find unreasonable and unacceptable.

You cannot always be good. You are human and have weaknesses. Stop judging yourself too harshly. Allow yourself some slack. Stop constantly blaming yourself. Accept that it's ok to be wrong/bad/moody/tired/confrontational. **This does not make you a bad person. It makes you normal!**

"God is paying me back"

This is a popular assumption to make when you life turns upside down. Not true – he is a loving God. God accepts you are a sinner and loves you despite your sins.

"I can't keep a relationship"
Can't you? Who said?

It takes two people to make a relationship work and if one isn't actively engaged in making the effort, it will become unhappy, and possibly end.

Relationships are like investments. 'The more you put in, the more you'll get out.' Similarly, the account can become overdrawn if you take more than you give.

At the start of a relationship you are always 'on good behavior': you are trying to show your best side and lure the unsuspecting significant 'other' to you. Everyone does this. We are all guilty of at first showing our best side and putting our best foot forward. Then what happens is that 'familiarity breeds contempt.'

Step 2 – Why Is This Happening To Me? 21

You become sure of your new partner and start 'taking the other person for granted.' This process is slow at first until eventually you stop listening to your partner; you begin manipulating situations and conversations in order to get your own way; you become complacent and resist catering to your partner's needs. These stages usually take a long time to manifest. Before you realize what is happening you are quarrelling, pouting, bullying, ignoring and making someone very unhappy by your actions and words. You become stuck in a rut of your own making. You must remember that your partner is probably doing the same thing.

The successful partnership will be able to identify the process taking place and will be able to discuss openly together the changes they see before them. Together they are able to recognize and change the pattern that has materialized and adopt different ways to deal with issues.

The unsuccessful partnership will be unable to communicate and will inevitably 'lock horns' on issues believing that each one is right and convinced that the other partner needs to change their ways in order to resolve the situation. They reach a 'watershed' in their relationship and, unless they both come to their senses and see what is happening, the situation between them will just get worse.

Step 3 Fear of the Future

Let's take a look at some of your potential fears:

- Being alone
- Surviving on little money
- Lack of trust for future relationships (although you firmly believe at this stage that you will never have another one)
- Being on the rebound
- Managing the children alone for the majority of the time
- Being taken advantage of by others
- Scared of tackling a variety of situations that usually you share with your partner — No one to protect you
- Dependency on family and friends

This is a list that can go on and on.

Let's examine some of these issues:

Being alone

You are not alone. You probably have an extended family also friends who care for you. You might have both children and a job. Therefore, you would have work colleagues who will be supportive also.

Perhaps you are totally alone with no children to consider. Perhaps you are unemployed. If these two issues apply to you and you are feeling depressed, isolated and alone may I recommend the help of a Counselor/Therapist to assist you through this difficult time.

Being alone is a state of mind. You can change the program in your mind to 'Not being alone.' You need to see your situation as it is and not as your old pattern of thinking believes it is. Look around you, are you really alone? How hurt would your family and friends be if they thought for one second that you believed that thought? Of course, we have to acknowledge that you can feel lonely when in a room full of people. In the early stages of a separation this is how you will feel. As previously stated, you will be imprisoned in your own thoughts.

That stage will pass—just hang in there and make sure you try to disengage from your negative thoughts and remain in a positive place and optimistic. This is hard to do I know but with practice you can achieve this state of mind.

Some people don't understand how you can be lonely if you have children to care for. What they don't realize is that as much as you love your children they cannot replace the love between a man and a woman. These two loves do not vie for first place in your heart—one doesn't necessarily come before the other. The two loves are different and you want both.

Surviving on Less Money

When a partner walks out through the door, money becomes an issue!

- Will s/he continue to support me?
- Can I afford two lots of rent?
- What can I do without?
- What can I do myself to improve my finances?
- How will I cover debts they have left behind?

Step 3 – Fear of the Future

Will s/he continue to support us?

Everyone's financial circumstances are different. You will or should know what your partner earns. If you do know then you can calculate the figures to reassure yourself that, providing s/he is responsible and reasonable and accountable, you won't have too much to worry about with regard to your finances.

If you are both unemployed, then the state will change your benefit to accommodate your new circumstances.

Perhaps your partner has moved in with someone, (lover, friend, or parent). If this is the case, then they will, obviously, have to contribute to that household but this amount wouldn't be nearly as much as if they would have to rent/purchase a home of their own.

Hopefully you both will be able to talk about this issue and come to an amicable settlement. If this cannot be done (both/or one of you, too angry, hostile unforgiving), then you will have to seek professional help from a Lawyer/Solicitor who can advise you of your rights.

You both might be in employment and earning a decent wage. What happens then? If this is so, an option could be to put an equal amount (taking into consideration your differing salaries) into a separate account for the sole purpose of maintaining the same standards, (for the sake of the children) as before the split. In my experience this option usually starts well, but ends up with one party withdrawing support eventually. Clearly, the best option is to have your finances professionally drawn up so that there can be no future debate and withdrawal of funds.

What can I do without?

Unfortunately for some, luxuries have to be abandoned after a split. For example you may need to deal with fewer or no meals outside the home; fewer cinema outings; limited expenditure for clothes, toiletries, petrol, chocolates, cigarettes and sweet things, etc. You have to 'pull your belt in' to ensure that there is enough money to last you until the next lot of money arrives.

When you are in these circumstances, you will be surprised to find how much money you used to waste in the course of a week. You will become aware of your spending like never before. You will assess the situation before you make your purchases and buy only what you need, not want. The phrase: **'When does a wish become a desire, become a want, become a need?'** fits aptly during this time of readjustment.

However difficult it seems, believe me you will adjust to your new financial circumstances. You will become prudent with regard to your financial affairs.

The positive aspect in this situation is that when you learn to successfully budget, you have a newfound power and control of your own money and your life. You don't have to check with anyone prior to spending. It is up to you. You will make mistakes, everyone does. Mistakes are learning curves. Without mistakes there is no learning. Remember, 'Rome wasn't built in a day,' forgive yourself errors on the path to getting it right. **You will get there.**

Step 3 – Fear of the Future

What can I do to improve my finances?

If you have family support, you could consider either part or fulltime employment. This break-up in your relationship might give you the opportunity of starting a new career or training/education for a career in the future.

Often family and friends rally around at these stressful times and may give help whenever or wherever needed.

If you have no nearby family and friends cannot assist you, then you might consider working from home. Look in the job vacancies section of your local paper to seek out employers who want help with tasks that can be accomplished from your home. They are out there—they do exist. Remember that legitimate work-from-home schemes never require fees to apply or start.

If you have children, you could also offer to baby-sit friends' children in order for them to have evenings out. (You might as well look after extra children because you have to look after your own anyway). Even if you did this a couple of times a month it all adds up to helping you out financially.

If you are a man reading this and need extra cash perhaps you could offer to do some gardening or handyman jobs for your friends at a reasonable rate. Moving out of the marital home has placed you in the position of having to purchase new furnishings and appliances.

Take a good look at your skills and identify how you could use them productively. The extra money you earn will help you finance seeing your children on weekends and having a good time with them

Another option might be 'bar work.' If you are the one caring for your children you could find a babysitter a few evenings a week in order to do this work. This has the twofold advantage of giving you an extra income and it would enable you to meet new people in pleasant surroundings. Who knows you may even get a date or two. Perhaps, if you are a man this would afford you the opportunity of meeting a divorcee with children of a similar age to yours who could play together. This would be an advantage financially as it is expensive taking children to places of entertainment on a regular basis. There are possibilities to earning extra cash—keep a lookout and don't disregard any options you may have at this time.

Being on the rebound: Lack of trust for any future relationships

You must not let future relationships suffer because of your past relationship.

You will of course be ultra-cautious, and that is only natural. You don't want to be duped twice, do you? You might think you will never be able to trust again. Perhaps you are right. Don't forget people have to earn trust; it does not materialize automatically. You are right to be cautious—you feel you cannot afford to make any more mistakes in relationships.

Now is the time to decide how you are going to approach a new relationship.

- Should you tell your new person about your past?
- What should you expect from a new person?
- Do you pay for yourself?
- If you are a man, should you foot the bill?
- How soon should you have sex with this person?
- It has been a long time since you have dated – you don't know what to say or do

Step 3 – Fear of the Future

Should you tell your new person about your past?

In my opinion you should only reveal what you want to. The information you give out should be on a 'need to know' basis only. When you begin a new relationship, you might usually tell the new guy/gal everything in glorious Technicolor™.

You confide all your insecurities, your sensitivities, your past relationships, how you were hurt; how you were treated, how you reacted, what you dislike most, and how someone can rob you of your self-esteem and self-worth etc.

Wrong! You might regret the information you are now revealing at a later date. What you are actually doing is giving the new guy/gal a comprehensive catalogue and insight into your weaker vulnerable self. This information could be stored by this new lover to use against you in the future. So be warned and be careful.

Of course you will say that you are separated or divorced, but if questioned further merely say that the relationship had come to a natural conclusion and you were both ready to 'move on.' During the 'getting to know you' period, this is enough information to impart. Later on in the relationship, you might want to say a little more. But remember, whatever you divulge is going to be put into your lover's memory bank for use when needed at a later date. Some might say that this is a cynical approach to new relationships. I disagree with that opinion: "A still tongue keeps a wise head." In my experience the less you say the better the relationship. You don't want to bring heavy, excess baggage into a new relationship do you?

You have been there and done that, for goodness sake let's move on with as little personal baggage as possible. Remain an enigma to some extent.

I am not suggesting you become Mata Hari or James Bond, I am merely pointing out that too much information given out during this vulnerable time can be detrimental to your relationship and mental health in the future.

What can I expect from a new person/lover?

You must decide what you want from your new lover. I can make these suggestions:

- S/he should be someone who is honest/fair and non-judgmental
- S/he should be attentive and considerate during the day and especially so at night
- S/he should be interesting to talk to
- You should feel proud of this person (after all your choice reflects who you are)
- S/he should be understanding
- S/he should be in regular employment (this does not apply to a woman who is raising a family)
- S/he must not be stingy with his/her time and money
- Neither should s/he be a spendthrift
- S/he must accept your children (if there are any)

This list is endless. You should consider carefully what you want in your life for the future. Remember, when you are choosing someone you are not just choosing a person but a way of life.

Step 3 – Fear of the Future

You are looking for someone who is honest and non-judgmental

Essentially you are looking for someone who accepts you for who you are. Don't be tempted to give this new person the impression that you are anything that you are not. If you paint a colorful picture of yourself, you are in danger of putting too much pressure on yourself to live up to the image you have created. We all want to come across as interesting and experienced, but resist the temptation to overstate your accomplishments.

The first point I made, in the above list, is '**you would like him/her to be honest.**' That might seem contradictory to my earlier suggestion that you tell him/her stuff on a 'need to know' basis only. So, to explain further, what I mean is that you can be honest about the stuff you are prepared to reveal, but keep the 'bad stuff' to yourself. Don't reveal what has the potential in the future to hurt and upset you. (This particularly applies to women).

Women are notorious at 'spouting forth' all the garbage they have experienced in past relationships. It doesn't do you any good to impart all this information in my experience.

S/he should be attentive and considerate during the day and especially at night

In the honeymoon period of a relationship, your lover will ensure that your needs are met. S/he will be loving, caring, understanding and will make you believe that they are "The best thing since sliced bread." But think on!

When you 'make love' you both will try and anticipate and satisfy the other person's sexual desires. The sex will be fantastic (you hope) and you will be delighted that this person cares enough about you to make sure that you are satisfied sexually.

- If you are a woman reading this, make the most of this honeymoon period. When you know each other longer and your relationship is more established, there is a distinct possibility that the focus will go from satisfying you, to satisfying himself

- If you are a man reading this, make the most of this honeymoon period. When you know each other longer and your relationship is more established, there is a distinct possibility that her focus will be on 'doing' it as fast as she can to get it over with.

- This sexual chemistry can last forever if you are both able to openly discuss your sexual needs and not feel embarrassed or rejected if you make a comment on what you want him/her to do. **Intimacy between two people is the most wonderful experience you can have, if you are with the right partner.** If you can look at each other wherever you are and intuitively know what your partner is feeling and thinking and you both want to accommodate the other person, giving the very essence of yourself then you are a **WINNER.**

S/he should be interesting to talk to

New sex is great but I believe you need more than that to have a lasting relationship with someone. Good sex with someone can fool you into thinking that you love everything about them. You don't notice their annoying habits. You don't see the flaws (at a later date they will be enormous to you.) If you enjoy talking with your lover and more importantly find him/her interesting and knowledgeable then you have the makings of a solid foundation to build upon.

Step 3 – Fear of the Future

I am not saying that your new partner has to be a budding Einstein or Madame Curie, I am just telling you that ordinary behavior, what they say, what that they do, says more about a person than how he/she performs in bed.

You should be proud of this person

If you are proud to introduce your new lover to family and friends, you will not only feel self-confident you will emit an aura of self-worth.

I am not talking about being proud of someone because they have come in first place on a TV quiz show. I am saying that you should be proud of the person they are: how they treat you, how they treat others, etc. The person you choose to spend the rest of your life with says a lot about who you are. It shows how much self-esteem you have.

S/he should be understanding

If you have to explain what you mean every time you open your mouth to speak, then the other person is lacking in understanding and probably not interested in what you have to say. Again, in the early stages of a romance you don't notice these things. They seem small and inconsequential. Believe me in the long run a lack of understanding between the two of you will be a massive hurdle to jump.

S/he should understand your family circumstances and cater to these facts. S/he should notice and be understanding if you are tired unhappy doing too much etc. If these issues are not understood by your new lover then ditch him/her. In all probability they will never have the capacity to understand what's going on and you will have to explain everything to them for the duration of your relationship.

S/he is in regular employment

If you are a woman reading this book then I am sure you will agree with me that it would be an advantage if your new lover had regular employment. **'Love on the dole'** doesn't work. You will eventually start bickering and arguing about money issues and the new found love will 'fly out of the window.' Again I am not suggesting s/he should be a 'Rocket Scientist' merely that a regular income is preferable and more conducive to a lasting relationship. A lazy partner is something you can do without.

If you are a man reading this and your new lover is raising a family, you will know and understand that in all probability she is living within a tight budget. Also, she cannot work unless there is someone to care for her children.

If however you are a woman who is fully employed and earning more than a living wage you will ascertain quickly whether or not your new lover matches your income and you will proceed accordingly.

S/he must not be stingy with his/her time or money

When a new relationship gets off the ground, you should expect your new lover to give you his/her time, get to know you, what you think, how you feel, and be sensitive to your needs and wants. If your new lover doesn't give you these things during early courtship, the chances are s/he will never give them to you later on. If your new lover cannot provide you with these basic needs during this early period, then it might be safe to say that s/he is primarily concerned with themselves and their own wants and needs. To love someone is to be unselfish in thought, word, and deed. The single best thing you can do when you have a new lover is to give them your time and treat them well.

Step 3 – Fear of the Future

'The formula for happiness and lasting love is each person putting the other partner first.'

Children

It is very important that your new lover should accept your children. This is essential for a harmonious future together. If one or other partner cannot accept and enjoy the other's children, then your relationship is doomed to failure. If this is the case and if **you** are the one with the children you will feel uptight and stressed when you are all together at the same time.

You will become resentful toward your new lover if you see them not involving your children in your relationship or if they ignore or admonish them.

Many children can be jealous and spiteful towards a new partner and this can have a negative effect on the new relationship. It is essential to bring a new partner into the relationship slowly and carefully. Your children have just experienced going through a traumatic period in their lives and their feelings should be a priority. Also, make a resolution that your children will only meet the new partner if you feel this partner will be longstanding. The meeting of too many potential partners will make the children feel insecure. You will expect your new lover to realize and understand that the child/children will always come first.

A mother's love is very different to the love she has for her partner. **No one comes first in this scenario, there are no losers.** However a new partner must appreciate that the children's needs will come before his needs. **They are after all children and you are both adults.**

If the new man in your life has children you should understand that his children might be confused and upset at another woman taking their mom's place. During times of access to his children, you should be prepared to take second place in getting his attention. In my opinion, becoming a friend to his children in the first instance is the best approach for the future.

If you are a man moving into a woman's home that she shares with her children, be respectful of their space. They might compete with you for their mom's attention. They might feel angry towards you for taking their dad's place. Understand that they are new to this process of readjustment and be aware and alert to the non-verbal displays of resentment they may exhibit. If you stay alert to the possibility of this happening you will be able to address this issue quietly, quickly and competently. If you are unable to do this successfully you could seek support and help from a Counselor/Therapist or even close members of your new partner's family and friends.

Step 4 The Grieving Process

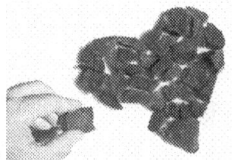

The following are the different stages in the grieving process, whether it is a death or divorce.

- Shock
- Numbness
- Disbelief/Denial
- Tearfulness
- Guilt
- Anger
- Giving in and giving up
- Fear
- Reliving memories
- Seeing your partner through rose-tinted spectacles
- Loneliness

These stages are in no special order. At any one time you can jump from tearful to lonely.

In some ways a divorce/separation can be much worse that losing someone through a death. I know that sounds ridiculous, but if you really think about it a dead person is no longer around; they are not **with** someone else; they have not dumped you for another person; they have not had enough of living with you; they are **DEAD**.

When someone you love dies, you can take flowers to a graveside and spend time there thinking and talking to your loved one. If someone you love dies after a long illness, then somewhere in your mind you are somewhat prepared for the death. You will go through the grieving process, but without the added dimension of feeling betrayed, abandoned with the knowledge that the person you love is living with someone else or prefers to be alone rather than with you.

On the other hand, when your lover walks out you will probably see them from time to time enjoying themselves with a new partner. You will see them picking up the children of the partnership (if there are children). You will have a constant reminder minute by minute that they are spending their precious time without you.

If someone you love dies suddenly (accident, heart attack, etc.) then you will not be prepared and will need time to come to terms with the death and you will be on the path of the grieving process.

The grieving process is a necessary time for you to come to terms with the loss of a loved one. It usually takes about two years of 'normal' grieving. You will experience the 'annual events,' such as, birthdays, anniversaries. For example, you will think this time last year you were going through the illness with your loved one; then the anniversary of the death and funeral. When you have experienced these significant days the mind begins to accept and prepare to 'move on.'

The first three stages of the grieving process I have identified are easily explained. Guilt, however, might need some clarification.

Guilt

When someone walks out on you the danger is to blame yourself entirely. This is not usually accurate. Remember, it takes two to quarrel and two to decide to part. It is, however, a natural response to someone you love not wanting you any-

Step 4 – The Grieving Process 39

more. You feel responsible for some (or all) of the breakup of your relationship.

You relive circumstances and situations that led to the split-up. You imagine handling these times differently and wonder if you had handled them in another way perhaps you wouldn't have come to the decision to break-up?

Your mind goes around in a whirl of self-hatred. Guilt can lead to depression and/or anxiety, as you mentally relive your life with your partner.

At this time, try to be realistic. Focus. See the past in a clear way. Check your thoughts and drag yourself from feelings of guilt back into reality. Even if you had an affair and this led to the eventual breakup, it is unlikely that another person would have attracted you sufficiently if things had been 100% fine at home.

Anger

You are angry that your partner has walked out. You may be left to manage the children and household affairs.

- Why should you be put in this position?
- What have you done to deserve this?

If you are a woman and your partner has moved on to someone else, you will feel angry that whilst he has been loving someone you have been slogging away, washing, ironing, cooking, cleaning and seeing to the needs of the children.

If you are a man reading this, then you will feel aggrieved that all the help and support you gave your partner has been thrown back in your face. You might be angry that you have been left alone and unloved having to start afresh with the rental or purchase of a new home, household appliances, furniture, etc.

In this instance, anger can be a positive emotion. It can spur you on to a more appropriate and powerful place in your mind. It can motivate you to putting the past behind you and starting your life afresh. You can think, 'I'll show you that I don't need you,' and, 'You just watch this space.' In my experience, anger expressed at this time dissipates rather quickly and once more you are plunged to the depths of despair. However the anger will return and it will feel like a huge fire inside you. This fire must burn out before you can truly break free from resentment.

You might want revenge. I have heard many revengeful stories. Some are quite elaborate and inspired.

Example:

"Hell hath no fury like a woman scorned."

One lady, after being, unceremoniously, dumped by a partner, proceeded to order a truckload of manure from a Garden Centre to be delivered at his new home with his new partner. Not content with this action, she drove to his house and parked the car in a spot that allowed her full vision of the scenario about to unfold. Soon, the lorry drove up and began unloading its contents all over the perfectly manicured lawn at the front of the house. Her ex-partner's new woman rushed out of the house to remonstrate with the truck driver only to be confronted with the recently abandoned woman driving by making rude signs!

I am not suggesting that this behavior is right or a good thing to do. It is not a good idea to react in this way.

Step 4 – The Grieving Process

Giving in and giving up

When you are living through this difficult period in your life, you believe that the easiest option is to 'give in and give up.' You can't be bothered with anyone or anything. You stay wrapped up in a cocoon of your own making believing that it's safe to huddle there. Thinking through and dwelling on your past has exhausted you and robbed you of the vital energy you need to live. Life can become a drudgery and you question the validity of your existence.

Example:

Ann was going through a separation or divorce. She awoke very early in the morning made herself a cup of coffee and smoked cigarettes endlessly until it was time to wake the children and get them ready for school. After the children were dressed, breakfasted, and taken to school she would crawl back to her empty bed and hide there until it was time to pick the children up from school later that day. Ann relied totally on her mother to clean the house, purchase and supply food, and amuse the children. She relinquished her duties in the sincere belief that she was a useless person.

Ann was, in normal circumstances, a very positive and happy person until her relationship broke down but soon after her husband walked out she was reduced to a physical and emotional wreck.

This period of 'giving in and giving up' continued until Ann's mother was rushed into hospital suffering from severe burns from an accident. Ann was forced to engage in life again and reestablish herself in the household. Even when this happened, it still took a neighbor and friend of her mother's to point out—none too tactfully—that Ann's home was dirty and untidy and this included Ann's personal cleanliness. It was the short, sharp shock Ann needed to pull herself together.

Frequently, it's even worse for a man, who may well lack housekeeping skills altogether. He may be unable to cook, know what to buy, how to mend clothes, etc.

Fear

Fear is a barrier that you have to surge through in order to achieve self-esteem. There are a number of fears:

- Fear of responsibility
- Fear of accountability
- Fear of success

Fear of Responsibility

Responsibility is being able to take control of your life. It means that you are:

- Whatever you think
- Whatever you feel
- Whatever you do

You are responsible for your children. You are responsible for what happens to you in your life. You are in control.

Fear manifests itself when you dwell on the bad things that have happened in your life. You must remember that whatever you have done in the past, you did with the knowledge and information you had at that time. **Don't waste time thinking of the past, you are not going in that direction.** Focus on the here and now, your future is ahead of you and can be anything you want it to be so decide now to embrace the future with hope and determination. Don't sabotage yourself by being self-critical and

Step 4 – The Grieving Process

judgmental. Know that if you decide on a course of action there will be an outcome. Understand that you will make mistakes. If you don't make mistakes you will never learn anything. The majority of learning comes from mistakes and the ability to move on and tackle the same action in a different way.

Fear of Accountability

The dictionary definition of accountable is, 'to be answerable to someone or something.'

In the first instance we are answerable to ourselves. Being answerable to yourself is achieved by living to a set of rules and regulations that you feel comfortable with.

The rules and regulations are made up of your beliefs behavior and responses to everyday living. You cannot hide from being accountable; it will catch up with you at a later time.

Fear of accountability lies in the uncertainty that you can live up to the self-imposed rules and regulations you have chosen to adopt. Accountability puts pressure on you to live by a certain standard and if you drop those standards you become disappointed in yourself. Your rules and regulations are not necessarily the same rules and regulations that other people live by and it is this that separates you from everyone else. The frightening aspect of accountability is that you may not comply with your peers. We all want to get on with each other and have an easy life and it is your own accountability that can distinguish and separate you from the crowd.

Your rules and regulations may be very different from those rules and regulations that you were raised by. As an adult you decide how to lead your life and the pattern of the past need not prevent you from acquiring a more suitable and appropriate code for living.

Fear of Success

Often you are afraid to try just in case you might actually succeed. You may always have believed that you cannot succeed; that a good life cannot be yours that there are winners and losers and you are the latter. Then the prospect of succeeding is scary and you may feel you are unworthy of achieving success.

Success is possible for all of us. In order to succeed, we have to leave old fears and thought patterns behind and accept that we all play on a level field and opportunities are there waiting for us. You deserve success as much as anyone else and it is there waiting for you. Don't let your old belief system prevent you from claiming the success that can be yours.

Ask yourself:

- Are you happy with you?
- Do you want to change your past pattern and adopt new rules and regulations that are more apt?
- Are your old patterns holding you back?
- Are you ready for the change?
- Do you know what new rules and regulations you want to adopt?
- What purpose will your new rules and regulations fill?
- Finally, are you satisfied that you have looked at the options and decided on a new set of rules that best gives you the structure you need to live by?

Step 4 – The Grieving Process

Remember that any change of patterns has an effect on those around you. You will have to allow sufficient time for those people close to you to adapt to your new outlook and new way of life.

Reliving Memories:

Unfortunately it's par for the course to relive the memories of your life with your partner. This is a particularly difficult time. These are some typical examples only of the memories you will be reliving:

- Memories of when you first met
- Your first kiss
- Birthdays
- Christmases spent together
- The first time you made love
- Meeting parents
- Integrating with families
- Getting engaged
- Getting married
- Honeymoon
- Your early life together
- Buying/renting a home
- Furnishing and decorating the home
- Shopping together
- Planning a family
- Pregnancy
- Birth of your first child
- The joy of parenthood
- Anniversaries

Once again, the list is endless! You will trawl through these memories and they will break your heart. It is necessary, however, to go through your memory box. It may be more comfortable to do this with a trained Counselor who can guide you and provide a structure to this process.

Seeing someone through rose-tinted glasses

Why is it that try as hard as you can you cannot remember the bad times in your relationship? All the bad situations you have had with your partner seem to have evaporated into thin air. This is most annoying to experience. Of course you had bad times (probably more bad than good if you were to be honest) so where are they?

During this phase you can rely on family and good friends to remind you of instances that now elude you. Good friends are very good at remembering the bad times and will at the drop of a hat recall them in detail. Momentarily this will make you feel good, but not for long. Try as you might to stop loving your partner you are unable to accept it right now. You are so sorry that this has happened—you didn't really think it would happen. You continue to believe that you still love him/her; that there is still a chance for you both. You give serious thought to whether you should both have stayed together for the sake of the children? The answer to this I believe is NO. Children pick up tension and anxieties. Instinctively they know if things are not right. Being honest with your children is in most cases is the best option.

If you are a woman reading this, the next time you see your partner (when he picks up the children), or out in a 'pub' you may feel a surge of anger and want to confront him with stuff you want to 'get off your chest.' There may be a scene and one of you will storm off (or be asked to leave the establishment) or you may burst into tears and want to persuade him/her to return. Whatever happens, you will end up in tears.

If you are a man reading this, you will be more likely to react to the same set of circumstances with either rage or spiral down into a depressive state.

You miss the silliest things about your partner the small stuff a person does that the other finds endearing. You never said anything about it at the time—you didn't think you needed to. On reflection, you think that perhaps you should have? Life is so unfair.

Loneliness

The loneliness you feel after a separation is overpowering.

The definition of this word from Webster's dictionary is, "cut off from others, sad from being alone, a feeling of desolateness."

"Loneliness and the feeling of being unwanted is the most terrible poverty," is a well known saying by Mother Teresa.

Judy Garland said, "If I'm such a legend, then why am I so lonely? Let me tell you, legends are all very well if you've got somebody around who loves you."

What are the feelings we may get when we are **not** in a relationship?

- Feeling Rejected
- Feeling Unloved
- Feeling Unwanted
- Feeling Ugly
- Feeling Bored
- Feeling Unworthy

- Low Self-Esteem
- No Confidence

Why is it that if you are **not** in a relationship you feel a failure? Why do you need someone else to validate you? When we **are** in a relationship, many of us let our friends go by the wayside and become exclusive to that one special person. We all want to be wanted and loved. It is human nature from the very beginning 'Adam and Eve.'

Remember that people who are in relationships can feel just as lonely as everyone else. Loneliness is the emotion you feel when you are emotionally cut off from those closest to you. It is a powerful emotion. The saying "no man is an island" suggests that you should maintain family relationships friends and personal relationships for the sake of your mental health. If all these relationships are maintained and you still feel lonely then you can safely say that your emotional needs are not being met. Research shows that any person, even an extreme introvert, needs identification with at least three social groupings. Loneliness can cause depression/suicide.

Things to do

- Set yourself unachievable goals.
- Set yourself goals that inspire you.
- Instead of 'slobbing out in front of a weepy film,' invite friends around for a girly/manly (playing cards, watching football) night in.
- Be proactive and meet new friends.
- Resist from reaching into the cookie jar; eat healthily and look after yourself instead.
- Seek out the company of other people.
- Drink only moderately.

Step 4 – The Grieving Process 49

- Enjoy your new found freedom. Be excited with the possibility of meeting a new woman/man.

What are unachievable goals?

They are goals that are too ambitious and way out of your reach. When you decide on your long-term goal set yourself achievable targets along the way in order for you to be able to clearly identify your progress.

What are goals that lack inspiration?

If your goals lack **passion** you will find that aiming for them will sap your energy and strength. In order to find the energy you require to achieve your goals you have to be focused, determined, driven, inspired, and enthusiastic. If you are all of these things then you will have a better chance of reaching your desired outcome. You need these emotions in place in order to sustain your vision of where you want to be. If your goal is uninspired and you lack the necessary enthusiasm in order to reach it then you will give up and opt out.

Inspirational goals are those that identify your passions

There are steps you can take at this time.

When there is a separation between couples the days and times you feel the emptiness most is during evenings and weekends particularly Sunday. For most people, Sunday is a quiet day with nothing much going on which gives you plenty of time to dwell on your loneliness and missing your partner.

Decide to do something about it, here are some suggestions:

- Visit family
- Visit friends
- Go to cinema

- Take a walk
- Redecorate your home
- Involve your children in a game, project, or trips to the park
- Make this day the day when you do your household food shopping
- Find a hobby
- Join a Society/Group/Organization

I am sure you can add to this list...

Things not to do:

Don't do a Bridget Jones and slob out in front of a weepy film.

The Bridget Jones film highlighted what many of us do when we are **not** in a relationship. We put out negativity and get back negativity. Bridget Jones behaved like a victim and a 'poor me'. She felt sorry for herself. She wallowed in self-pity. She recognized some of the things she was doing wrong, e.g., over-eating over-drinking but did very little to redress the balance. She believed that she needed someone else in her life to provide her with love happiness and contentment.

Don't be a victim or a 'poor me'.

Who wants to be around a victim or a poor me? Think of the people you know (and we all know them) who are constantly moaning about their misfortunes. They personally are out of control and their lives are out of control. They perpetuate the poor me syndrome and expect nothing good to happen. They have not put into place structures or boundaries that would help them in their life. If you live in this haphazard state, you will have little self-respect or self-esteem. What you are actually say-

Step 4 – The Grieving Process

ing about yourself is that 'you can treat me how you want to because I do not think I am worth more.' Knowing your structures and boundaries will help you gain self-esteem. This is because these rules highlight both to yourself and to others the way you treat yourself and the expectations you have of how you want others to treat you. If none are in place, you are putting no value on who you are or what you want.

Don't replace a relationship be eating lots of food (comfort eating).

Replacing love with food is a common occurrence. You dig deeper into the junk food and lavish a ridiculous amount of food on yourself. The non-verbal communication here once again is that you are unlovable and have given up.

- You eat because you feel in a low mood
- You eat because you are stressed
- You eat to aid relaxation
- You eat because you are bored with everything
- You eat because it gives you something to do

Eating for these reasons is habit forming and is another indicator of low self-esteem. This behavior forms a pattern and can lead to health problems. You eat because you are unhappy, not because you are hungry. You are substituting food for the love you have lost.

You should aim for some progress every day, however small. Take time out to notice and record your progress. Keep a journal. Reward yourself for the progress you have made and forgive yourself the mistakes you inevitably make. Progress should make you happy with yourself. If it is not making you happy then perhaps you should reevaluate your goals.

The Two Questions Everyone Should Be Asking:

- Are you making good progress toward your long-term goals?
- Are you enjoying the progress you are making?

As Robert F. Kennedy (1925-1968) once said: "Only those who dare to fail greatly can ever achieve greatly."

Step 5 Acceptance and Realization

Slowly the penny is beginning to drop. Or put another way you are no longer living in 'never-never land.'

- You have pined for your partner
- You have regretted the split up
- You have hated and blamed yourself
- You have hated and blamed your partner
- You have hated and feared the future alone

You have been on a treadmill going around in circles and regurgitating the same stuff for too long. You become:

- Sick of yourself
- Frustrated with yourself
- Angry with yourself
- The whole situation exasperates you

All these things brought together identify that you are accepting the situation as it is and are preparing to move on, mentally and physically. You want to close your eyes and skip the next few months/years and reach a place where you are happy.

Don't forget that you only really learn from stuff that goes wrong in your life.

Take a risk

Start changing by taking baby steps. Take a small risk. Step out of the box that hems you in and dip your toe in the water of your future life. You can start in a very small way by rearranging the furniture in your home. Moving furniture around will help you to stop reminiscing about your past, e.g. (that's his/her chair, s/he decorated the living room). If you can afford it, redecorate your living room, buy new cushions, and move the ornaments to a different place. Throw out the old and bring in the new. This action will help you cast out old negative patterns. Empty your drawers and throw out useless stuff you have been hoarding for years. Use this time to make your home – **YOURS!** Co-opt the help of family and friends and enjoy changing things around you. All this is a positive step toward a new future.

If you are the one forced out of the family home, now is the time to start afresh. Become excited and interested in where you would like to live and what furniture you want, etc. Create a living space that reflects who you are.

Acceptance

Accepting yourself and where you are in recovering from your ordeal is an important stage in successfully emerging from a break-up. Accepting yourself enables you to move on from your current state. In order to **accept**, you must be able to understand the journey so far in coming to terms with the changes in your life. You have experienced painful times during this process, but are now ready to accept what has happened.

You are in the 'Acceptance' stage if you agree with statements like the following:

- When you accept the situation you are in, and are beginning to allow changes to take place
- When you wake up each morning and the first thought isn't about your ex-partner
- When you begin to feel good about yourself
- When you become happy most of the time

Step 5 – Acceptance and Realization

- When you don't need anyone else to validate who you are
- When every day doesn't feel like a month
- When you feel motivated to move on from the past
- When you feel you can make decisions (however small)

All the above are crucial in realizing that you are indeed moving through this period in your life.

Step 6 Family and Friends

Your Support System

Family and friends will notice the change in your thoughts, speech, and behavior during this process of change. They will probably welcome the change and should support and encourage you. Particularly at this time, these people will help you by reinforcing your positive thoughts about your future and will confirm your negative thoughts about your past.

- You have accepted that you cannot turn back the clock
- You will hope that the children have come to terms with the situation. However some children take a long time to accept a new set of circumstances and they may still hope that their parents will get back together. This issue takes time, patience and understanding with continual support from both parents
- You will see that you are not so tearful
- You will see that your finances are sorted out
- You will identify that you can budget
- You will see that this split-up is not the first thing you think about upon waking in the morning
- You will see that the split-up is not on your mind 24/7
- You will begin to socialize
- You will start enjoying your life again

'You have climbed this mountain with a heavy heart, but now are ready to make a fresh start.'

Step 7
Moving On

The Ladder of Recovery

In order to move on, it has been necessary for you to climb the ladder of recovery. It hasn't been easy for you, remembering and examining your life with your partner. Not so long ago you were spending all your time thinking about him/her and it used to upset you.

Now you find that

- You don't think about him/her so much
- You haven't got the constant picture in your mind of your partner being intimate with someone else
- Your mood has calmed down and you don't feel constantly angry any more
- You might now feel that this other person (if there is another party involved) is welcome to your partner
- You now see your relationship with him/her realistically and might have come to the conclusion that it was right to part when you did
- You ask yourself if s/he wanted to come back to you, would you want that? **You have answered NO.**

You have been through the experience of yearning and wanting to know every single thing your partner was doing. Now you aren't bothered.

- You are no longer interested in what s/he are doing
- You understand that you have dwelt on your ex-partner's life for far too long
- You accept that if s/he has found someone else, or even if they haven't but have moved out anyway, then clearly they didn't value you, love you, or respect you anymore

This is a good place to be. The cloud has shifted from above your head. The days are sunnier. You are optimistic yet realistic about the future. You are still scared, of course, but the fear is something you now understand and accept. You may now begin to understand the concept of 'life is about taking risks.' For some people, however, this does not happen and they are left in a void, unable to move on. If this is the case then you should ask for the help of a Counselor/Therapist to assist you in moving on.

Moving on may suggest to you that you leave all the past behind you. This need not be so. Take the good things with you and put them in your good memory drawer. Learn from the bad things and place them in a drawer; lock the drawer and throw away the key.

Throughout this whole new experience of letting go of the past and developing a plan for the future, you will be assisting your children to move on also. This task will need careful handling. The memories they have of you both are precious to them, and you might experience sleepless nights whilst they come to terms with their loss. One thing to remember is not to say bad things about the other parent. This also applies to the partner who has left the home. It is important that your children know that you both still like each other and are seen to be getting on with each other as this can help to make your children emotionally stable.

Step 7 – Moving On

To be able to let go of the pain and upset the sense of betrayal, and to move away from the sense of loss and emptiness you need to find a way of putting all that behind you and rediscovering your new future your new way of life.

Step 8 Reinvestment / Restructure

Finding New Goals

Ask yourself who and where do you want to be in 2 or 5 years? In chapter 4, The Grieving Process, I refer to the importance of setting goals. Below are some examples.

- You want to let go of bitterness
- You want to be happy
- You want your children to be happy
- You want to own your own home (if you don't already)
- You want to take time out for yourself
- You want to have a good social life
- You want to learn something new
- You want to get a satisfying job
- You want to own who you are, and be proud of your accomplishments
- You want to learn to ask questions, without making accusations in those questions
- You want to learn to say NO

This is an exciting time. You are reestablishing and reinventing yourself. The sky's the limit.

When you embark on a new relationship without realizing it, you become someone else. You slowly change to become someone you intuitively feel will meet your new lover's wants. On a subconscious level you take on board the things your new lover says and on an unconscious level you adapt accordingly to meet this new person's needs and wants. I believe that this happens more to women than to men. Women are generally more flexible and can more easily adapt to new situations. Of course, this does not happen to everyone but it certainly happened to me. We do this without knowing it. A few months or years into the relationship you find that you do not recognize yourself anymore. What have you become? Who are you? The person you once were wouldn't tolerate what you are experiencing in this relationship and yet here you are putting up with stuff and you can't remember when or how you changed.

This new situation you are in is an opportunity to reclaim who you once were. Or it can be the path to becoming the person you want to be.

You are now in control of you life. You can and should put into place how you want yourself and your life to be. You have choices to make, e.g.:

- How to spend your time
- Value what you are doing
- Decide not to be a slave to household tasks or the job
- Find a job that you will enjoy
- Search for the right Educational/ Retraining Course/ part-time job
- Be in mutually respectful relationships
- Acknowledge that you will need support
- Be emotionally independent (not needing someone else to make you and your life happy)
- Learn to prioritize (and accept that you can' do everything)
- See the funny side of life and go with the flow
- Don't look back — look to the future

Step 8 – Reinvestment / Restructure

How to spend your time:

You accept that you are a busy person. However you must acknowledge and accept that time set aside for you is of the utmost value. I believe that if your own needs are met, then all those around you will benefit. If your needs are unmet everyone suffers as you become more and more unhappy and depressed. Set aside time each day just for yourself. During this time you have the option of watching the television going for a walk doing some form of exercise listening to a relaxation tape. **Switch your mobile phone off and spend some quality time doing nothing much.**

Value what you are doing

Whatever it is you are involved in enjoy the moment and value your input. Recognize your strengths and accept your weaknesses. You cannot be good at everything so don't worry about the stuff you are not so good at. People will notice the difference in you during any changing process. Don't let this stop you from being who you want to be. Be brave. If you can manage financially without getting a job and want to be a stay-at-home Mum/Dad, that's great. Don't let the opinions of others stop you from doing what you want to do. You have considered the options and chosen what you want to do.

Decide not to be a slave to household tasks

Learn to cut corners wherever you can, i.e., ask yourself, 'do I need to do that?' If the answer is no, don't do it and don't feel guilty about it either. Do you really need to iron tea cloths/socks/towels, etc? It's up to you how much or how little you do. You can free yourself up to do anything you want. Enjoy.

Find a job you know you will enjoy

If you decide to get a job don't rush in where angels fear to tread. Proceed carefully and research all areas well before you decide what you want to do. Look at the advertisements for jobs in your local newspaper and see what takes your fancy.

Educational/Training Courses

If you think you would like to retrain visit your local college and make enquiries about what's on offer. Join an evening class. Search on-line for possibilities. Take your time in order to assess your next move accurately.

Be in mutually respectful relationships

Whilst you need to stay alert and aware of people and their possible motives, you must afford your new partner the trust you expect them to give you. It is important not to bring your past baggage into your new relationship. We all learn from our mistakes, but we also learn that life without taking educated risks is unproductive and static. When taking a new partner into your life, you will be constantly learning about them and their opinions on every issue. This is good as it stops you taking things people say on face value alone. It gives you the opportunity of looking deeper into your new relationship and from that standpoint you can decide if and when you want to react. At this time in your new relationship you can take stock before you commit yourself to anyone or anything.

Acknowledge you will need support

If you are a perfectionist start loosening up and chilling out and you will find looking after a new family more rewarding and enjoyable.

Step 8 – Reinvestment / Restructure

If you are a man without a family to look after, you have the opportunity of reinventing yourself. Set targets and goals that reflect what you might have wanted in the past but had to put aside as not practical living within the set up you have just left.

If you are a man joining a ready-made family, take your time to blend in and be accepted. Learning to live with a ready-made family is difficult and should be approached in a careful responsible way.

Don't try and do everything simultaneously because you may flag and fail and then get upset with yourself. Your family might be able to help out with support or you could have help from other parents in the same position as yourself. Don't be afraid to admit either to yourself or to others that you need help. Loneliness and isolation are two of your worst enemies. To acknowledge you need help is not a sign of weakness. It is a sign of strength.

Be emotionally independent

Don't rely on someone else to make you happy. Most of you will have experienced emotional dependency. Dependency can range from a romantic attachment to a platonic relationship that has become almost obsessional. It develops from having a low self-esteem and little confidence.

Dependent vs. Healthy Relationships

How do you recognize that you are in a Dependent Relationship?

- If you are angry, jealous, or depressed when other people are involved with this person
- If your focus is entirely on this relationship to the exclusion of others

- If you need to see this person every day
- If you feel you must check with his person before taking a step in life
- If you only feel safe and secure when in this person's company
- If you need this significant other to be focused on you
- If you need this significant other to spend most of their time with you
- If you get angry when left out of social occasions (even if the social occasions wouldn't interest you)
- If this person can upset you by a glance or turn of phrase

A break-up is an emotional, vulnerable period to live through. If this break-up has brought on a depressive state then, it's possible for you latch on to one or more people who can give you the insight you need to move on. During this time it is easy to become dependent on someone you admire and respect if you perceive them as being strong and independent. You want to be like that person. You feel safe in their company and are prepared to listen and act on what they say. This happens because you don't trust your own instincts anymore. Your confidence is at an all time low and you are afraid that you will make the wrong decision. Therefore you rely on someone you respect to show you the way and act as your guide. This dependency can also occur when you have been bereaved, lost your job, moved to a new area at University, etc. This is not unhealthy in itself. However problems occur when we have a desperate need to have them around most of the time.

Step 8 – Reinvestment / Restructure

How do you recognize a Healthy Relationship?
- If the relationship is equal
- If you both have personal freedom
- If you both feel safe when apart from each other
- If you respect each other
- If you acknowledge and accept your differences
- If you can engage in a healthy debate
- If you are both able to change your mind without causing distress to the other
- If you can say NO without causing distress
- If you trust each other
- If you have both decided to put each other's needs first

It would be wonderful if we could have all the above. However let's be realistic—if we had it all that would be utopia wouldn't it? It is something positive to strive for in a new relationship.

Priorities

It is important to prioritize so that you won't get flustered or become disabled with too many things going around in your mind. You can get confused with information overload. So what should you do?

- Make a list of all the things you want to achieve
- Being objective, make another list from the first one, of the things that need urgent attention. (I don't mean the ironing or housework.) This is what you can change now, e.g., put into place family support or

crèche facilities for your children, whilst you retrain or get a job
- Set yourself achievable targets in order to reach your long-term goal
- Set yourself a realistic time scale for these targets
- If you feel in a rut at the moment, do something different. Give yourself permission to be flexible. Give yourself some time-off, if necessary. Be kind to yourself
- Learn to put yourself first (it's hard to do this but you will see the benefits)
- Learn to adjust to new thinking and behavior patterns

See the funny side of life

If you can laugh with a new partner about personal issues then your relationship has a good foundation to build upon. You may be able now to stop yourself from arguing even when you disagree with someone reasoning that the issue is not that important. You are developing your new character learning about life and how to successfully live with others.

Look around you at other people and see if you can identify whether they have humor in their lives. If you can see a discussion or an argument getting serious and you have no real feelings about it you can end it by agreeing with them saying YOU ARE RIGHT ON THIS ISSUE. If you are able to do this you are learning to differentiate between important issues and inconsequential stuff.

Step 9 — Look to The Future

How do you plan a future?

- By deciding what you want
- By setting rules and regulations that you are comfortable to live with
- By daring to take risks
- By thinking outside the box
- By valuing yourself
- By believing in your ability to change your life
- By being unafraid to make mistakes
- By learning new things
- By learning new thought patterns
- By learning new behavior patterns
- By learning to react appropriately
- By learning to be flexible
- By learning to reconsider when this suits you
- By being honest with yourself

Deciding what you want:

By the time you have reached this chapter you may be ready to move on from your recent static sad state. I have outlined in previous chapters that to move on you need to identify what you want in your life.

- Write down your long-term plan
- Write down your short-term plan
- Write down your achievable targets in order to reach your short-term plan

This simple exercise will help to de-clutter you mind and this will enable you to visualize your targets more easily.

The next stage in deciding what you want is to list the advantages that you will achieve when your targets are reached. Focusing on the results you want will help to motivate you towards reaching them. Anticipate setbacks and plan how to overcome them. Being well prepared will assist you when things go wrong. Decide to 'Never give up!' If you feel low, read the advantages you have written down and that you will benefit from and this action will energize you to press forward. Getting support and surrounding yourself with positive people will help you move forward with your plan.

Listen to your inner thoughts and dare to make your private dreams a reality. Ensure that your goals are achievable and realistic. Don't be afraid of failing. When babies learn to walk they fall down all the time but they never give up they simply try, try, try again. This is a process we all learn by.

Step 10 A New You

Learn to see your mind in a different way.

See your mind as a toolbox and your thoughts as tools. If your tool box is messy and your tools blunt and broken how will you ever create anything that looks half good?

Instead, tidy your toolbox and sharpen your tools (in other words clean up your mind and correct your thoughts). A process takes place in your mind before an action takes place.

The process is:

- First comes a thought
- Your mind accepts the thought
- Your mind then produces a feeling
- Then the feeling provokes an action
- An action takes place

This process occurs to everyone. To explain further, if the thought is:

- I will never do that
- I can't win
- There is a constant black cloud over me
- I am useless
- I will never amount to anything
- I am unlovable
- I am a bad parent
- I am unemployable
- I can't make good relationships

...then the feeling you experience is a negative one. It disables you. You are unable to try anything new believing that you will never achieve it. You can change this pattern of thinking by becoming aware of your thoughts and correcting them before they get to the action stage, i.e.,

- Stay alert and recognize the thought
- Work through this thought and envisage the outcome you always arrive at (most repeating patterns have regular repeated outcomes)
- Ask yourself if the outcome is based on concrete evidence (i.e. If you have a fear and have confronted the fear did you pass out/faint/injured yourself?)
- Ask yourself what would the outcome of the same thought be if arrived at logically
- Now look at the same thought again and find a logical and realistic outcome. (This is a general outcome that most people would think of)

When you have done this and are satisfied that your original thought was produced through a bad thinking habit and fear the next stage is to:

- Stop the thought immediately
- Put a positive thought in it's place (in other words a realistic, normal outcome)
- Experience a change from a negative to a positive feeling
- Accept that a new action is about to happen

Relaxation and meditation techniques will help you to achieve this new process. You will need to practice thinking positive thoughts. It will be difficult at first, but with continued practice you can acquire this positive process.

Step 10 – A New You

Another useful tool is to write out a four line mantra. These four lines should be positive and focused on what you want for your future. A suggestion is:

> 'I am as good as anyone else.
>
> I can get what I need
>
> I am looking forward
>
> I expect good things to happen.'

By repeating this mantra every day, you will be sending positive messages to your mind to reprogram your thoughts and actions. This technique tells your subconscious mind that you have already changed and expect good things to happen. This change in your thinking process will attract positive people, opportunities, and situations into your life. Be proactive. Find out whom you need to contact what is it that you need to do? Take steps toward your target.

New relationships

I have already suggested some characteristics you may want to look for in a new partner. Remember you will be afraid of taking a risk with someone new. You have experienced bad things in your former relationship and undoubtedly will completely believe and vow that you will not put yourself through all that again. That is normal. Everyone who has gone through a separation and divorce makes that promise to themselves.

Also remember that your new partner will bring his/her excess baggage into the relationship. This person will also be cautious of a new relationship. S/he won't want to jump in at the deep end. S/he will in all probability have their guard up against being hurt again. So be aware of his/her hang-ups.

Making significant life changes is a very difficult process. Having made some of these changes you certainly don't want to return to your old patterns and experiences in a new relationship.

Take your first step in a new relationship by allowing it to grow in a healthy way—give it time to develop. This will give the relationship a good, solid foundation. Treat it tenderly with careful nurturing.

Steps to find a new relationship

- Change your social routine
- Accept invitations to parties/evenings out, etc
- Decide what sort of man/woman you are looking for
- Do you want a short or long term relationship?
- Be open-minded—but stay well clear of engaged and married men/women
- Stay alert and observe a likely person's behavior toward you and others
- Make sure you remember the rules and boundaries you have decided upon
- Don't rush headlong into an intimate relationship. You will know when the time is right
- Be happy and do your best to relax and enjoy this time

Step 10 – A New You

I hope this poem I have written will help you as you step out to your new future

Letting go of the past

The time has come to let go of the past
It's been hanging around you, keeping you fast
Tied to your pain and feelings of guilt
Tied to rejection, unable to quit
It holds you so close
You just cannot let go
You want to be free
You hate yourself so

You turn a corner
You're lighter in step
Freedom is coming
You'll get there yet!
Open your heart
Let the good feelings flow
Rest in this place and bathe in the glow

Thank God you've arrived
You are in the right place
Stay where you are
Don't be in haste
Good times are coming
This is your time
Enjoy your new freedom
And accept the divine

Lynda Bevan

About the Author

Lynda Bevan lives in a picturesque village in South Wales, United Kingdom. She is 59 years of age, married for the third time, with three (adult) children. During her teens and early twenties she pursued and enjoyed acting and taught drama at local Youth Centers.

Her 22 year career has involved working in the area of mental health, with the two major care agencies in the UK, Social Services and the National Health Service.

After the birth of her third child, and with her second marriage ending, she became employed by Social Services and climbed through the ranks to senior management level with some speed.

During her career with Social Services she developed a passion for counseling and psychotherapy and worked extensively with mental health patients within the organization, setting up counseling projects in Healthcare Centers. The task was to tackle the issue of doctors who inappropriately referred patients to Psychiatric Hospitals for therapy when they had experienced events that arise in normal everyday life, e.g., divorce, anxiety, depression, bereavement, stress, loss of role. It was during this time that she became involved in marital/relationship counseling and, coincidentally, was experiencing difficulties within her own relationship. The experience of working in this environment, and her own relationship issues, enabled Lynda to be innovative; creating methods of coping and developing strategies that enabled her and her patients to live within their problematic relationships. These strategies were devised and offered to patients who had clearly identified that they did not want to separate or proceed with the divorce process.

About the Author

After taking early retirement from Social Services, she became employed by the National Health Service as a Counselor in the Primary Healthcare Setting. During this period in her career, she began using the strategies she had developed with patients who were referred for relationship counseling and who did not want to end their partnership/marriage. These strategies have been used extensively over a ten year period with impressive results.

Lynda is presently employed as a Manager of a charity that supports people who are HIV positive. She is also the Resident Relationship Counselor on Swansea Sound Radio.

Bibliography

Dyer, Dr. Wayne W. (2004) *The Power of Intention*, CA, USA Hay House Publications,

Hay, Louise (1984) *You Can Heal Your Life*, CA, USA Hay House Publications

Hicks, Esther and Jerry (2004) *Ask and It Is Given*, CA, USA Hay House Publications

Jeffers, Susan (1987) *Feel the Fear and Do It Anyway*, USA 1988 – First Ballantine Edition

Lama, Dalia, Howard C. Cutler (1998) *The Art of Happiness*, New York Riverhead Books (Penguin Group USA) Inc.,

Norwood, Robin (1985) *Women who love too much*, New York Jeremy Tarcher, Inc., of the Putney Berkley Group

Peck, M. Scott (1978) *The Road Less Traveled*, New York Arrow publication.

Rampa, Tuesday Lobsang (1990) *You Forever*, USA Samuel Weiser, Inc.

Rampa, Tuesday Lobsang (1956) *The Third Eye*, USA Brandt and Brandt

Redfield, James (1995) *The Celestine Prophecy*, New York, USA- Time Warner Publication

Ruiz, Don Miquel (2001) *The Four Agreements*, USA Amber Allen Publications

Ruiz, Don Miquel (2002) *The Mastery of Love*, USA Amber Allen Publications

Index

A

accountability, 43
alone, being, 23
anger, 7, 8, 37, 39–40, 40, 46
anti-depressant, 12
anxiety, iii, 4, 7, 39
apathy, 7
ashamed, 4

B

being human, 18
belief system, 44
Bridget Jones, 50

C

cheating, 19
children, 12–16, 27
    and finances, 15
    and new partner, 35
    behavior after split-up, 14
    bond with parent, 13
    living with one parent, 14
    resentment of new partner, 36
    self-esteem of, 13
    staying together for, 46
confidence, 11, 48, 67, 68

D

denial, 8, 37
depression, 4, 7, 39, 48

E

eating, 50, 51
employment, 25

F

fear, 37, 42, 74
    of accountability, 43
    of making the wrong choice, 7
    of responsibility, 42
    of success, 44
    of the future, 4, 7, 23–36
finances, 24–28
    cutting back, 26
first night alone, 4

G

Garland, Judy, 47
giving in and giving up, 37, 41
goals, 48
good behavior, being on, 20
grieving, 3
    separation vs. death, 37
guilt, 7, 37, 39

H

hate, 7, 8
honesty, 15, 31
honeymoon, 31

K

Kennedy, Robert F., 52

L

loneliness, 37, 47, 49

M

mantra, 75
marriage
    as a contract, 10
meditation, 74
memories, 45

N

negative emotional experience, v
numbness, 37

O

over-eating. *See* eating

P

partner
   left you for someone else, 8
   new, 21, 35
partner who leaves
   feelings, 2
passion, 49
plan, 72

Q

questions
   unanswerable, 1, 10

R

rebound, 23
relationships
   new, 76
   starting new, 28
remembering bad times, 46
remorse, 4
revenge, 2, 40
role models, 13

S

self-care, 7
self-confidence, 4
self-critical, 42
self-esteem, 29, 33, 42, 48, 51, 67
self-hatred, 39
shock, 37
sleep, 6
success, 44
suicide, 48

T

thoughts, stopping negative, 74
trust, 23

U

unlovable, 11, 19, 51

V

victim, being a, 50

Y

yearning for the past, 3

Life Skills:
Improve the Quality of Your Life with Metapsychology.

"I recommend this book to anyone who's setting out on their personal life's journey and adventure. I rate Ms. Volkman's book 5 stars!"
—Lillian Caldwell, Internet Voices Radio

Life Skills, by Marian K. Volkman makes use of one-on-one session techniques to achieve the individual's personal goals -- from relieving past pain to living more fully to expanding consciousness.

▫ Learn handy and usually quite fast techniques to assist another person after a shock, injury or other distress.

▫ Learn simple methods for expanding your awareness on a daily basis.

▫ Gain a deeper understanding of what a relationship is, and how to strengthen and nurture it.

▫ Learn the components of successful communication, what causes communication to break down, and how to repair breakdowns.

▫ Learn an effective tool for making important life decisions.

Praise *for Life Skills*

"*Life Skills* is replete with examples, exercises, episodes from the author's life, and tips—this is a must for facilitators, clients, and anyone who seeks heightened emotional welfare—or merely to recover from a trauma."
—Sam Vaknin, PhD, author of *Malignant Self Love: Narcissism Revisited*

"*Life Skills* is a serious, impressive, and thoughtful work with one objective in mind: teaching how to reach one's full potential in practical, pragmatic, easy-to-follow steps that will literally change one's life." —James W. Clifton, M.S., Ph.D.,

"*Life Skills* by Marian Volkman is not to be read once and then put away. It is a guide to living a full, satisfactory life, a philosophy, a challenge. If you take the trouble to do the exercises the way the author suggests, they will change your life."
—Robert Rich, Ph.D., M.A.P.S., A.A.S.H.

Loving Healing Press 5145 Pontiac Trail
Ann Arbor, MI 48105
(734)662-6864
info@LovingHealing.com

180 pp trade/paper ISBN-13 978-1-932690-05-7— $16.95

Includes biblio., resources, and index.

http:/www.LifeSkillsBook.com

Beyond Trauma:
Conversations on Traumatic Incident Reduction, 2nd Ed.

"Not in 30+ years of practice have I used a more remarkably effective clinical procedure."
—Robert Moore, PhD

Victor Volkman (Ed.) takes the mystery out of one of the more remarkably effective clinical procedures in a way that can help millions of people revitalize and improve their lives. To those desperate people who have experienced trauma or tragedy, this process is a pathway to dealing with their feelings and getting on with their lives

In the new book **Beyond Trauma: Conversations on Traumatic Incident Reduction**, Volkman presents a series of conversations with a wide range of people from many different backgrounds and experiences. Each provides his or her perspective on Traumatic Incident Reduction, or TIR for short.

Readers will learn about how TIR has helped domestic violence survivors, crime victims, Vietnam vets, children, and others.

Praise *for Beyond Trauma*

"Beyond Trauma outlines the elements with clarity and insight as to how TIR will resolve wrestling with dilemmas, understanding your demons, and climbing out of emptiness."
    —Sherry Russell, Grief Management Specialist and Author

"Our staff therapist is finding Beyond Trauma very helpful".
    —Joan M. Renner, Director, Sexual Assault Program, YWCA of Clark County, WA

"Beyond Trauma: Conversations on Traumatic Incident Reduction is an excellent resource to begin one's mastery in this area of practice."
    —Michael G. Tancyus, LCSW, DCSW, Augusta Behavioral Health

Loving Healing Press
5145 Pontiac Trail
Ann Arbor, MI 48105
(734)662-6864
info@LovingHealing.com
Dist. Baker & Taylor

Pub. March 2005 — 360 pp
trade/paper — 7"x9"
ISBN-13 978-1-932690-04-0
$22.95 Retail
Includes appendices, bibliography, resources, and index.
For general and academic libraries.
http:/www.BeyondTrauma.com

Exclusive offer for readers of *Life After Your Lover Walks Out*

Share the power of Loving Healing Press Books
Order direct from the publisher with this form and save!

Order Form – 15% Discount Off List Price!

Ship To:

_____   ☐ VISA   ☐ MasterCard   ☐ check to
Name   Loving Healing Press

_____   _____ _____/_____
Address   Card #   Expires

_____   _____
Address   Signature

_____ _____   Life Skills   ____ x $14.50 = _____
City   State
                                     Life After Your... ____ x $15 = _____
_____ _____ _____
District   Country   Zip/Post code   Beyond Trauma ____ x $19 = _____

                                                    Subtotal = _____
_____
Daytime phone #   Michigan Residents: 6% tax = _____

                                     Shipping charge (see below)   _____
_____
email address   Your Total _$_____

Shipping price <u>per copy</u> via:

☐ Priority Mail (+ $3.50)   ☐ Int'l Airmail (+ $4)   ☐ USA MediaMail/4th Class (+ $2)

Fax Order Form back to (734)663-6861 or
Mail to LHP, 5145 Pontiac Trail, Ann Arbor, MI 48105

www.ingramcontent.com/pod-product-compliance
Lightning Source LLC
LaVergne TN
LVHW011428080426
835512LV00005B/323